FAR FROM HOME

CATH SENKER

W
FRANKLIN WATTS
LONDON•SYDNEY

Franklin Watts

First published in Great Britain in 2017 by The Watts Publishing Group

Copyright © The Watts Publishing Group 2017

Editor: Amy Pimperton
Art Director: Peter Scoulding
Designer: John Christopher/White Design
Cover design: Peter Scoulding
Picture Researcher: Diana Morris
Picture credits:
Mohamed Nureldin Abdallah/Reuters: 24. Action Press/REX/Shutterstock: 52t. Anwar Amro/Getty Images: 22. Brian Atkinson/Alamy: 13t. Ali Atmaca/Anadolu Agency/Getty Images: 28b. Baltimore Sun/Getty Images: 14t. Max Bryan/Alamy: 39t. Elsa Buchanan/IB Times UK: 11. danielo/Shutterstock: front cover © DDP USA/REX/Shutterstock: 4. Michael Debrets/Pacific Press via ZUMA/REX/Shutterstock: 38. Dan Derheimer: 15. dikobraziy/Shutterstock: front cover t. Nick Economou/Shutterstock: 8, 35t. Joseph Eid/AFP/Getty Images: 23t. Pascal Fayolle/SIPA/REX/Shutterstock: 48. Findlay/Alamy: 55t. Gregor Fischer/DPA/Alamy: 32b. Janossy Gergely/Shutterstock: back cover t. Gonzalesphoto/CityPress24/PAI: 50. Martin Hanzel/REX/Shutterstock: 57. Maja Hitij/AFP/Getty Images: 47. Hossaini/AP/REX/Shutterstock: 54-55. Chris Huby/Le Pictorium/Alamy: 26. Arantxa Hurtado/www.bohemianlight.com: 42. IBL/REX/Shutterstock: 51. Andrej Isakovic/AFP/Getty Images: 52b. Jordan Pix/Getty Images: 6. kafeunkolik/Shutterstock: 17. Irina Kalashnikova/SIPA/REX/Shutterstock: 39b. Anjo Kan/Shutterstock: back cover b. Isaac Kasamani/Getty Images: 10. Bullent Killic/AFP/Getty Images: 27. Eric Lafforgue/Getty Images: 9. Lina Lees/Shutterstock: 14b. David Litman/Shutterstock: 13b. Hussein Malla/AP/REX/Shutterstock: 43. Eugenio Marongiu/Shutterstock: 44b. Khalil Mazraawi/AFP/Getty Images: 20t, 20b. meunierd/Shutterstock: 49. Migrant English Project: 45. Emillio Morenatti/AP/REX/Shutterstock: 28t. Marwan Naamani/Getty Images: 16. Nice_Media/Shutterstock: 30, 31. Photoshot/Avalon: 58. Issouf Sanogo/AFP/Getty Images: 25t. Seita/Shutterstock: front cover b. Snowleopard1/Getty Images: 46b. Sam Tarling/Corbis via Getty Images: 19t, 23b. TASS/Getty Images: 7. 360b/Shutterstock: 40. © UNHCR/Shawn Baldwin: 21. © UNHCR/Mark Henley: 1, 32t, 44t, 59b. © UNHCR/Joel van Houdt: 36b, 37. © UNHCR/Andrew McConnell: 5. © UNHCR/Diego Ibarra Sanchez: 18-19, 63. © UNHCR/Roland Schoenbauer: 34-35, 62. © UNHCR/Achillieas Zavallis: 33. UPPA/Photoshot/Avalon: 59t. Pius Utomi/AFP/Getty Images: 12. vlada3/Shutterstock: back cover. Wllliam West/AFP/Getty Images: 53. jochem wijnands/Horizons EEP/TRVL/Alamy: 36t. Wikimedia Commons: 46t. Xinhua News Agency/Photoshot/Avalon: 56, Xinhua News Agency/REX/Shutterstock: 29.

Every attempt has been made to clear copyright. Should there be any inadvertent omission please apply to the publisher for rectification.

ISBN 978 1 4451 5519 7

Printed in Dubai

Franklin Watts
An imprint of
Hachette Children's Group
Part of The Watts Publishing Group
Carmelite House
50 Victoria Embankment
London EC4Y 0DZ

An Hachette UK company.
www.hachette.co.uk
www.franklinwatts.co.uk

The figures and statistics quoted in this book were correct at the time of going to press.

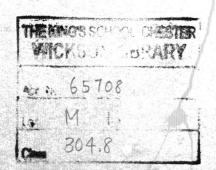

CONTENTS

RUNNING FOR THEIR LIVES

29 December 2015: With heavy hearts, Naleen and her husband Dara shut the door of their home in Kobane, Syria ❶, for the last time. With their little daughter Lamar and baby son Pulat, this Kurdish family embarked on the well-trodden route to Europe via Greece ❷. 'My children gave me the courage to leave. If I'd waited for Daesh [ISIS], they could have killed them before my eyes,' explained Naleen.

⬇ *A view of the destruction in Kobane, northern Syria, due to fighting between Kurdish forces and ISIS.*

THE LONG JOURNEY

After travelling through Turkey *and Greece, the family continued with a group of Arab and Kurdish Syrians to the Macedonian border. It was risky. Having arrived in Europe, they were supposed to claim asylum in the first safe country, but Naleen and Dara were heading for Germany or the Netherlands. Every time they crossed a border, they were breaking the law.*

Rather than relying on untrustworthy and expensive people smugglers, the family travelled with a group of fellow refugees, relying on maps on their phones. Walking day and night, they carried their children, turning off their torches each time a vehicle approached. Even little Lamar knew they were crossing borders secretly. 'We had to tell her to be quiet and not make a sound,' said Naleen.

From Gevgelija, Macedonia, they took a train and later walked through a forest they had heard was full of bandits waiting to rob them. They walked as quietly as they could, with young men on the outside, brandishing sticks for defence. The women were in the middle, gripping their children's hands tightly. Everyone was terrified, but they made it through the forest safely.

As the families crossed the border into Hungary, the police arrested them. They lost all their bags. After three horrendous days locked in an overcrowded, baking-hot cell, Naleen's family were released. But they were now alone. With no group support, they had no choice but to trust people smugglers to take them to the Netherlands; fortunately, they safely reached Ter Apel in the north of the country.

Use the map locators and the maps at the front and back of this book to find the location of places and countries mentioned in the book.

↑ *Naleen, Dara and Pulat on their lengthy journey to Europe.*

NALEEN'S HOPE

Naleen and her family were relieved to arrive in the Netherlands, but many hurdles still lay ahead. And for Naleen, 'other people's countries, no matter how beautiful or lovely, even if it is like heaven, will never be the same as our homeland.' One day, she hopes to return to Kobane in Syria.

ON THE MOVE

By the end of 2017, there were 25.4 million refugees worldwide – people forced to flee their countries to escape war and persecution. Most of them were in neighbouring lands. Of all refugees, 85 per cent are in developing countries.

⬆ *Syrian refugees, including children and elderly people, make their way to Za'atari refugee camp in Jordan.*

SYRIA TORN APART

After civil war broke out in 2011 between forces loyal to President Bashar al-Assad and anti-government rebel groups, hundreds of thousands of Syrians fled to Lebanon, Turkey, Jordan and Iraqi Kurdistan. When the radical Islamist movement, the so-called Islamic State of Iraq and Syria (ISIS), seized parts of Syria and Iraq in 2013–14, the crisis was renewed. To stem the tide, neighbouring countries introduced restrictions on refugees. Around the world, few countries offered lifelines to Syrians seeking shelter.

FLEEING TO EUROPE

Yet in 2015, even greater numbers fled: 1 million Syrians escaped by sea to Europe. ISIS remained a threat, but even greater dangers came from government barrel bombs and Russian air strikes. Western countries, led by the USA, also bombed Syria to target ISIS. Huge numbers lost their livelihoods, children could no longer attend school and one-third of the hospitals were closed. By February 2016, the Syrian Center for Policy Research reported that a staggering 400,000 Syrians had been killed in the violence.

Yet in March, the European Union (EU) tried to prevent more refugees from fleeing further into Europe by making a deal that allowed Greece to return them to Turkey. This did not stop people trying to escape.

MILLIONS ON THE MOVE

Such mass migration is nothing new, but we are seeing the largest movement of people since the Second World War (1939–45). This book focuses mainly on the refugee crisis in the Middle East, examining why people move, how they travel and what it is like for the survivors who find refuge and those who host them. Most importantly, it asks: is there a way out of the crisis?

SYRIAN REFUGEES IN THE USA

By November 2016, more than 13,000 Syrian refugees had been resettled in the USA. To help them integrate, they were placed in communities where Syrians were already settled. From January 2017, the new US president Donald Trump decided that the USA should no longer welcome significant numbers of refugees. In the past, the USA accepted large numbers of refugees fleeing crises, including more than 300,000 Vietnamese in 1979–80. Going further back in history, the USA operated an open-door policy towards immigrants from many nations until after the end of the First World War (1914–1918).

⬇ *A Russian fighter jet takes off from Hmaimim Air Base in Syria.*

WHY DO PEOPLE FLEE THEIR HOMELAND?

Most people have no desire to leave their homeland. Refugees are forced to flee while others make the difficult decision to leave to improve their chances in life.

⬇ *Traumatised Syrian refugees land on the Greek island of Lesvos after crossing the Mediterranean Sea from Turkey.*

The Yazidi people are a Kurdish group who have suffered persecution over hundreds of years.

ESCAPE

Refugees are people who flee their country because of war or violence or 'a well-founded fear of persecution for reasons of race, religion, nationality, political opinion or membership in a particular social group' (1951 Refugee Convention). Refugees are protected under international law and receive aid. In the 2010s, long-term conflict or human rights abuses have pushed people to escape from Afghanistan, Sudan, South Sudan and Eritrea.

Internally Displaced Persons (IDPs) flee for similar reasons to refugees, but remain in their own country. They do not receive the same legal protection as refugees. With the growing number of civil wars over the last few decades, the number of IDPs has risen steeply. By the end of 2017, there were an estimated 40 million. The countries with the largest number of IDPs in 2017 were Syria, Colombia, the Democratic Republic of Congo and Afghanistan.

A 'WELL-FOUNDED FEAR OF PERSECUTION'

Conflicts frequently involve racism against minorities or persecution on the grounds of ethnic group or religion. In Syria and Iraq, ISIS persecutes Assyrians because they are Christians, while in Iraq it punishes Yazidis, a Kurdish group with their own religion.

People may endure persecution because of their gender or sexuality. The Taliban is a radical Islamist group that controls parts of Afghanistan **7** and is a major threat to the government. Its members believe that girls and women belong at home and should not attend school or go out to work. Meanwhile, in Uganda, it is illegal to be LGBTI (lesbian, gay, bisexual, transgender, intersex).

"

If we sent the girls to school, the Taliban would beat them and carve in their leg with a knife [the words], 'This is what we will do if you send your daughter to school.'

Golpari, 23, Afghan woman, Katsikas Camp, Epirus, 8 Greece

9

CASE STUDY Ketifa's story

Ketifa and Sharon were 16 when they began their relationship at a boarding school in Kampala, Uganda 🎈. They loved each other, but they understood the risks. In their country, it is illegal to be LGBTI, and the punishment is a 14-year prison sentence – or worse. As Ketifa says, 'In Uganda, you grow up knowing being a homosexual is bad.'

One day, a classmate found one of their love notes, and the head teacher promptly expelled the girls from school. In their hometown of Mutundwe, the local community council met to discuss the accusation that Sharon was a lesbian. Ketifa kept out of the way. Hours later, she learnt to her horror that the meeting had ended with the participants beating her girlfriend to death.

Yet Ketifa was not discovered. She switched to a new high school, graduated and entered university in Kampala. Later, she began a relationship with a female classmate, and again was discovered. This time, the university dorm owner told her uncle. He and his friends punished her severely, by beating and raping her.

Severely traumatised, the following morning Ketifa fled to Kenya. She worked for a food vendor for three days to earn enough money to reach Kakuma refugee camp **10**. There, she joined a group of other LGBTI Ugandan refugees who supported each other. Yet in the camp, they endured homophobia from other refugees. Ketifa took a job as a secondary school teacher in the camp but soon the rumours about her sexuality led to complaints from parents. They pushed for the school to sack her and two gay Ugandan teachers.

↑ *'Charles' is transgender, identifying as female. Like Ketifa, she fled Uganda for her own safety.*

The LGBTI refugees were then sent to their own compound away from the main refugee camp, although this wasn't a perfect solution because other refugees were jealous of their slightly better conditions. Now they were living separately.

Ketifa wanted to be resettled in a country that would not discriminate against her for being a lesbian. Her refugee status was approved in 2016, and the following year she was accepted for resettlement in the USA. In November 2017, Ketifa finally arrived in Oakland, California.

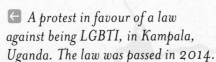

← *A protest in favour of a law against being LGBTI, in Kampala, Uganda. The law was passed in 2014.*

BLURRING THE BOUNDARIES

There are clear differences between refugees and migrants. Yet sometimes people leave as migrants but turn into refugees because of changing circumstances in their home country. Imagine a Syrian student who set out to study at university in the UK before civil war broke out in her country. At the end of her course, her student visa ran out, but owing to the conflict in Syria, she knew she would face danger on her return. Unwittingly, she had become a refugee. Realising the war in Syria was likely to continue for some time, she applied for asylum in the UK.

⬆ *In 2015, around 22,000 Nigerian migrants came to Italy, hoping for a better life. This Nigerian woman sews clothes for a living.*

THE IMPORTANCE OF DEFINITIONS

A refugee is clearly defined as an individual forced to escape war or persecution. A migrant is a person who moves to improve their lives. If people blur the definition and talk generally about waves of Middle Eastern 'migrants' coming to Europe, it takes attention away from the specific needs of refugees and can undermine support for them. In the 2016 crisis, the vast majority of people arriving on European shores were refugees. A very small proportion were migrants. Therefore the United Nations Refugee Agency (UNHCR) talks about 'refugees and migrants' when referring to these movements.

MOTIVATION TO MIGRATE

Some people are forced to flee, but there can be many other reasons why people leave their homeland. There may be problems in the migrant's home country, such as natural disasters, a high crime rate or a lack of public services. An individual might have difficulties, such as continual crop failures or deep poverty. Perhaps the economy is in crisis, so job opportunities are scarce, or instability and violence are common, such as in Central America. On the other hand, a richer country may have good land and a healthier environment, more and better jobs, an efficiently-run government and good public services, and a lower crime rate and risk of natural disasters. Generally, migrants move to a place where there is a higher standard of living. Eastern European migrants mainly go to western Europe, Mexicans tend to move to the USA and large numbers of Indians and Chinese people migrate to the USA and Australia.

⬆ *There are few opportunities for people who live in this poor area of San Pedro Sula in Honduras, Central America.*

⬇ *Many migrants to the USA find work picking crops at harvest time.*

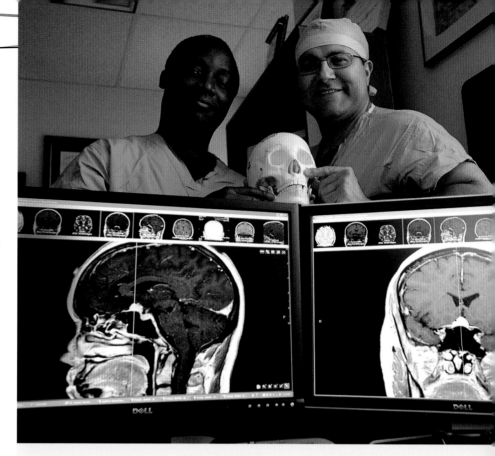

➡️ *Kofi Boahene (left) and Alfredo Quinones-Hinojosa (right) are both surgeons at Johns Hopkins Hospital in Baltimore, USA. Dr Alfredo Quinones-Hinojosa is a migrant from Mexico and Kofi Boahene was born in Ghana but moved to the USA to work as a doctor.*

⬆️ *The city of Perth on Australia's west coast is a popular choice for British migrants.*

SETTLING IN A NEW LAND

Migrants do not only move from poor countries to richer ones. Large numbers of people from wealthy western nations move to a new country to settle. They often relocate for a particular job; in the USA, an employer may sponsor a skilled worker they need for their business, paying to help the individual to come. Others migrate to join a spouse, parent, sibling or child. They have to apply for a visa, fill in many forms and go to an interview. Migrating to a new country is a long and complex process.

Hundreds of thousands have taken this option. The largest group of foreign-born residents of Australia are British – 4.1 per cent of the population in 2017. There are 310,000 British migrants in Spain, 280,000 in Ireland and 190,000 in France. Many of the British people moved to Spain because they preferred the warmer climate on the sunny Mediterranean coast, often living in communities with others from their country. Every year, thousands of US citizens move to Canada to settle, while thousands more migrate in the opposite direction.

FORCED TO LEAVE

In 2017, there were 258 million international migrants in the world. The majority had relocated to improve their lives, but more than 25 million were refugees. UNHCR reported that 'persecution, conflict, or generalized violence' had forcibly displaced a colossal 68.5 million people in total – including 40 million people displaced within their own country.

CASE STUDY A rich cultural life

Clare comes from London, UK **11**. After training as a violinist at the Guildhall School of Music in London, she and her American musician husband, Pete, moved to Seville, Spain **12**. They both found work with the Royal Symphony Orchestra of Seville and as music teachers. They learnt to speak Spanish fluently. The pair brought up their two children in Seville. Danny and Lucy are bilingual and have grown up absorbing Spanish, British and American cultures, celebrating festivals from each country. They join the Seville street festivities of Holy Week and dance at the April Fair, share American Thanksgiving with friends, and hang up stockings for Father Christmas, British-style, at Christmas. Clare still feels English, and her husband, American, but Spain is their home.

⬇ *Lucy, Clare, Pete and Danny, photographed at the Seville April Fair.*

REFUGEES IN THE REGION

⬆ *A Syrian labourer works on a construction site in Lebanon.*

Most people who have fled their homes are Internally Displaced People in their own country or refugees in neighbouring countries. The majority of Syrian refugees – more than 5.5 million – are in the Middle East, presenting huge challenges for their host countries.

⮕ *Turkish soldiers patrol the border with Syria to prevent new refugees from entering Turkey.*

FRUSTRATIONS FOR REFUGEES

Refugees often do not enjoy the same rights as citizens in the countries to which they have fled, so it can be hard to access homes, jobs, schooling and health services. In Turkey, refugees have the right to work, but only if the employer offers a contract and agrees to pay the minimum wage. Some Turkish employers particularly like to employ Syrians because they can pay them less than Turkish workers, so they frequently offer them casual jobs illegally with no contract. Until August 2016, Syrian refugees had to pay for work permits in Jordan, so they tended to work unlawfully there too. Although many Syrians are highly skilled and educated, the restrictions mean they are often unable to practise their professions and instead do low-paid building or cleaning work. It is frustrating for them and a huge blow to their sense of pride as well as their living standards.

DISPLACED WITHIN SYRIA

Being an Internally Displaced Person is similar to being a refugee. IDPs are still in their own country but have been forced to flee, leaving their home and possessions behind. By the end of 2017, there were 6.2 million Syrian people displaced within Syria. Most live with host families, in private accommodation or in makeshift camps. When the money they brought with them runs out, finding food, water and shelter becomes a daily struggle.

TURKEY: A STRAIN ON SERVICES

For the second year running, in 2015 Turkey hosted the largest refugee population in the world, most of them Syrians. Although many Turkish people were sympathetic to their neighbours' plight, the huge numbers put a strain on public services and led to complaints that the newcomers were taking locals' jobs. From spring 2016, Turkey began to illegally return thousands of refugees to Syria even though the country was still in turmoil. It introduced tight border restrictions, only accepting refugees at land borders who needed emergency medical care. Syrian refugees were therefore pushed into the hands of people smugglers to cross the border into Turkey.

CASE STUDY The 'lost generation'

Many refugee children lose out on their education, which affects their chances of a good career in the future. Often they have missed classes in their own country because of war – perhaps their school was bombed or it was too dangerous to leave the house. They may be on the move for weeks or months seeking refuge. When they arrive, there may be no school places for them or they have to study in a different language, so they fall behind. Sometimes they have to go out to work or look after younger siblings to help their family to survive.

Samir, 11, and Mohammed, 7, left Aleppo in Syria 13 with their parents in 2013 and fled to Beirut, Lebanon 14. The schools were so overcrowded that there was no space for them. The following year, they departed to Izmir 15, Turkey, where they had relatives. Samir was placed in fifth grade (Year 6) and Mohammed in first grade (Year 2). Because he was so young, it was easier for Mohammed to learn the language and fit in with others who were just starting school. The only Syrian in his class, he received excellent marks in all his subjects after the first year. Mohammed said, 'I like school – I have a good teacher and good friends who are very polite and respectful. I speak Turkish, not 100 per cent yet, but I am learning.'

In contrast, Samir could not follow his lessons and was behind in all his subjects because he had missed school since second grade (Year 3). He said, 'I felt very isolated. The other kids would mock me, but I didn't understand what they were saying. My teacher was nice to me but got frustrated because we couldn't communicate with each other.'

➡ *Some Lebanese schools have a second shift in the afternoon to allow refugee children to attend.*

Samir's father asked the teachers to put Samir in a lower class: 'We tried to explain how hard the language is for Arabs, but they said no.' Samir refused to continue at school and now works full-time with his father in a shoe-making workshop. Pushed into the adult world before their time, young Syrians like Samir have been called the 'lost generation'.

⬆ *This 10-year-old Syrian boy does not attend school. Instead, he shines shoes for a living.*

⬆ *Children help their family to make a living in Za'atari.*

MAKING THE BEST OF IT IN JORDAN

In Za'atari in northern Jordan **16**, international aid organisations and Syrian refugees have transformed the sprawling refugee camp into an orderly town with shops, services and decent security.

Around 80,000 Syrian refugees live in portable homes in Za'atari, which has become Jordan's fourth biggest city. It is run by UNHCR, the Jordanian government and more than 40 humanitarian organisations. Most of the refugees arrived with few possessions or money, and rely on food aid. Nearly a fifth are under five years old. Every person receives food vouchers worth about £11 a month to spend in Za'atari's two supermarkets. Most of the produce is grown in Jordan, so Jordanian producers benefit from sales. The World Food Programme runs a bakery producing bread for the camp, and all the bakery employees are refugees.

 *Back in 2014, Za'atari residents had makeshift stalls to sell goods. Since then, shops and restaurants have been established.*

WORK AND COMMUNITY

Around 5,000 people are working within the camp, and around 10,000 have work permits for jobs outside. Refugee doctors and nurses provide healthcare in the hospital and ten medical centres. The hospital is for the many trauma victims — people who have lost limbs in the war. Along the main street, residents have set up various small businesses selling clothes, shoes and bikes and offering phone repairs. The people of Za'atari have done their best to create a sense of community, just a few kilometres from their war-torn homeland.

A marriage takes place in a Jordanian camp. For many young girls who are living in camps, a good education is so hard to achieve that they opt for an early marriage instead.

CASE STUDY Khaldieh's Story

There are 29 schools in Za'atari, but only half the children go to school. Most 16–24 year olds in Za'atari are not in employment, education or training. Khaldieh Ali is one of the few young women with a job. Aged 18, she came to Za'atari with her family in 2013 and had to drop out of school because her father was worried she would be harassed by young men. Now she has high hopes of becoming a journalist. She writes for the camp magazine *The Road* and in 2016 became deputy editor of a new women's magazine, *Yasmin*. She told the *Jordan Times*, 'I want the world to know that we, Syrian children, have our own dreams and ambitions.'

This family fled from Palestine to Syria, then Syria to Lebanon. Palestinian Syrians are some of the poorest people in Lebanon.

SURVIVING IN LEBANON

Syrian refugees make up a quarter of the population of Lebanon yet, as registered refugees, they are often excluded from legal employment. They may only work if they buy an expensive residence permit – four-fifths of Syrians do not have one.

The Syrians seek the cheapest accommodation: in cities, rents are cheaper for the lower floors, where there is less fresh air and light. They often share a flat with their extended family or friends. Some homes are so overcrowded that people sleep in eight-hour shifts in a single room covered with mattresses, and those who are not in bed have to go out. It is common to eat poor-quality food, sometimes past its use-by date. People eat less too, especially women – they feed the men and the children first.

FRUSTRATIONS FOR HOSTS

The poorest people in Lebanon, who include Palestinian refugees, feel that the influx of Syrian refugees makes life harder for them. Palestinian refugees have limited rights to work in Lebanon; they are not permitted to work in 20 professions so they usually do manual labour (working with their hands). The Syrian refugees compete with Lebanese residents for jobs, and the Lebanese complain that employers fire them in order to employ Syrians on lower wages. Lebanese residents are frustrated that the Syrian refugees receive aid, which allows them to survive on smaller incomes. The large number of newcomers increases the demand for homes, and rents are rising, as are the prices of basic foods. It is the Syrian refugees who are blamed for all these problems rather than the landlords, who profit from the rents, and the employers, who enjoy reduced wage bills. The poorest Lebanese residents are hit the hardest by these imbalances in the economic system.

Syrian refugees live in this run-down apartment block in Lebanon.

OUTSIDE THE LAW

Many refugees have no choice but to work illegally. Wages are low and employers can hire and fire illegal labourers as they wish – there is nothing employees can do about it. If men cannot find enough work, boys as young as ten try to find a job. Women do not generally go out to work owing to fears for their safety. Families with no income borrow money and rely on help from charities.

SHARING RESOURCES

People help each other out if they can. If a sick person urgently needs medical treatment, everyone chips in. It gives a sense of community solidarity in difficult times and a feeling that not all is lost.

⬆ *Lebanese protesters march against a curfew (ban) that stops Syrian refugees from leaving their homes between sunset and sunrise, 2016.*

JOURNEY TO EUROPE

What is it like attempting to journey to Europe with no legal right to travel and no particular destination? It may mean a long and treacherous trip overland through the desert or a hazardous voyage by sea.

DANGERS OF THE DESERT

Sub-Saharan Africans pay a fortune to people smugglers and risk their lives crossing the Sahara Desert **17** to reach the Libyan coast. One route runs from Agadez in central Niger **18** to Tripoli in Libya **19**; in Agadez, people smugglers employ local drivers who know their way across the sands. The police turn a blind eye to the smugglers in exchange for bribes. The 4x4 trucks are filled with spare fuel and water and are packed so tightly with passengers that those on the outside have their legs dangling out of the vehicle.

← These migrants on their way to Libya have been caught by soldiers in a remote desert area of Sudan.

Another route runs from Khartoum in Sudan **20** to Ajdabiya in Libya **21**. Eritreans, Somalis and Sudanese people are crammed into lorries to travel hundreds of kilometres to Libya. The desert travellers risk dying of thirst if water supplies run out, abandonment if the fuel runs out, or robbery by bandits. Even if they make it safely to Ajdabiya, refugees are often kidnapped and held until relatives pay the ransom. If they refuse to pay, the refugees are tortured until their relatives do pay up.

Next, the refugees travel to Bani Walid **22** or another coastal town in sealed containers. This is necessary because they pass through ISIS territory, and if ISIS fighters discover the fugitives, they seize and kill the Christians.

↑ Migrants leave Agadez for Libya, packed on to pick-up trucks.

MAZRAA

The final waiting area is a *mazraa*, a smugglers' compound at Bani Walid, Zuwara or Garabulli near Tripoli. The travellers are held until their families pay for the next leg of the journey by boat to Italy. They may wait weeks or months in this hellish place, squashed into a tiny room with up to one hundred others, surviving on a ration of food once a day. Beatings are frequent, and many women endure rape. As an Eritrean doctor recalled: 'All the suffering that a human can suffer happens in this mazraa.'

BLACK MARKET

In Izmir, Turkey, a flourishing black market developed, selling goods to refugees hoping to cross by boat to Greece. An essential item for every sea traveller is a life jacket. Some refugees in life-threatening situations at sea have been horrified to discover that their life jacket was a fake that made the wearer sink rather than float. Who knows how many have died owing to this criminal trade?

⬇ *This shop in Izmir, Turkey, sells life jackets for children. It is impossible for desperate refugees to tell which are fake and which are real.*

CHANGING ROUTES

Until March 2016, a major refugee route to Europe ran from Turkey to Greece. Many thousands of Syrians crossed the border to Turkey, while Afghan refugees in Iran or Pakistan walked to Turkey. They then hoped to travel by boat to Greece. In 2016, Libya to Italy became the most common route.

ACROSS THE OCEAN

In the early 2010s, Izmir became Turkey's smuggling capital. Until 2016, the route between Turkey, Greece and the Balkans was simpler than trying to reach Libya and then Italy. It was possible to cross the Aegean Sea by boat from Izmir to a Greek island. From there, refugees went overland through the Balkans.

People smugglers control the business of bringing refugees across on boats from Libya and Turkey. For the Aegean crossing, dinghies are used; for the central Mediterranean route, smugglers mainly use old, unseaworthy fishing boats, which are cheaper than regular boats. They advertise their services on social media, making the trip look like a tourist outing. International governments have focused on trying to stop the smugglers, but they are hard to prevent. The main problem is not the existence of the smugglers but the demand for their services. While there are people desperate to flee, people smugglers will profit from their desperation.

NO GUARANTEES

Refugees may have sold their home and used all their savings to pay for the chance of a journey to safety. Even though they have paid a fortune to smugglers, there is no guarantee they will reach their destination in Europe. Putting your family in a flimsy dinghy when you know that thousands have perished on such crossings is a mark of true desperation. It is tragically common to hear Syrians say they feel dead already, so there is nothing to lose.

Refugees and migrants, whose boat is in trouble, wait to be rescued near the Greek island of Chios.

DANGEROUS DINGHIES

Inflatable dinghies are designed for short trips with a few passengers, not for crossing the ocean packed with men, women and children in every available space. An overcrowded dinghy can overbalance, and the people on the edge may fall in and drown; many refugees cannot swim. With no professional navigator to guide them, it is easy to get lost. The engine can fail, leaving the boat at the mercy of the winds and waves, or the dinghy may be shipwrecked far from shore in a storm.

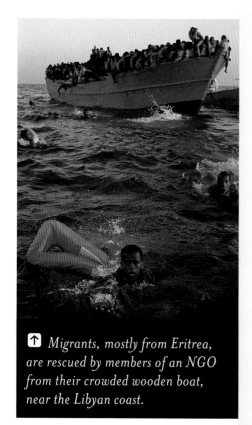

↑ *Migrants, mostly from Eritrea, are rescued by members of an NGO from their crowded wooden boat, near the Libyan coast.*

STAYING ALIVE

On board, the travellers do their best to prevent disaster. They keep as still as possible to avoid unbalancing the boat, and food and water are shared out according to need. The more confident take charge of navigation. Once close to land, a passenger phones an activist or the coastguards in their destination country. In emergencies, Non-Governmental Organisations (NGOs), such as Sea-Watch, run rescue missions. Sea-Watch volunteers work around the clock, and in all weather conditions. When they receive a distress call, they launch one of their ships, with rescuers and medical staff on board. Using GPS technology, they locate drifting craft and bring the refugees aboard.

↓ *A Turkish coastguard helps to rescue a baby from a sinking boat.*

CASE STUDY Act of heroism

Sometimes when things go wrong and no rescue boat can be contacted, only an act of heroism can save the dinghy. Eighteen-year-old Yusra Mardini is an Olympic swimmer from Damascus, Syria **23**. Training as war raged around her, she frequently found herself swimming in the open air because parts of the roof had been blown off the pool. She and her sister, Sarah, fled Syria to Lebanon, then Turkey. From Turkey, they departed across the Aegean Sea on a dinghy intended for six people – it was carrying twenty. After just half an hour, the motor failed. Yusra, Sarah and two other swimmers leapt into the water and pushed the boat for three hours until they reached the Greek island of Lesvos. Yusra recalls, 'I had one hand with the rope attached to the boat as I moved my two legs and one arm ... I had to be funny even though I was almost dead because there were two six-year-old boys on the boat and I didn't want them to feel like we were dying.' Yusra and the other swimmers managed to save the lives of all the people on the dinghy.

The sisters eventually reached Berlin, Germany **24**, where Yusra joined a swimming club. She trained daily before and after school. Yusra

⬆ *Yusra Mardini competed in the refugee team at the Rio Olympics, 2016.*

was overjoyed to be selected for the first-ever refugee team at the Rio Olympics in August 2016, and she won the first heat of the 100 m women's butterfly race. She used her prominent position to speak out for refugees: 'I want everyone to think refugees are normal people who had their homelands and lost them not because they wanted to run away and be refugees, but because they have dreams in their lives and they had to go.'

LIVING IN LIMBO

Refugees arriving safely in Italy or Greece are clearly relieved at surviving the journey and delighted to be in Europe. But they are exhausted. They may have lost family members or experienced terrifying journeys, and be suffering from post-traumatic stress disorder.

SAFE BUT ANXIOUS

In late 2018, conditions in the camps on the Greek islands of Samos **25** and Lesvos **26** were terrible. At Vathy on Samos, around 4,000 people were squashed into a camp intended for 650. Newcomers were housed in flimsy tents. There was no running water or electricity. Many of the toilets and showers were broken, and raw sewage spilled around the tents. There were rats everywhere.

Yet they had support from some local people and small community organisations. Refugee Support runs markets in Greek camps, giving everyone tokens to buy food and clothes.

WOMEN'S SAFETY

People living in the camps feel insecure, particularly women. In the stressful atmosphere, arguments and violence often break out, and sometimes women are attacked and raped. Tagrit, a Syrian woman, reported: 'We don't feel safe going to the showers or the toilets alone. We have set up groups of six and we all go together. If one wants to go, she has to take another five women with her.'

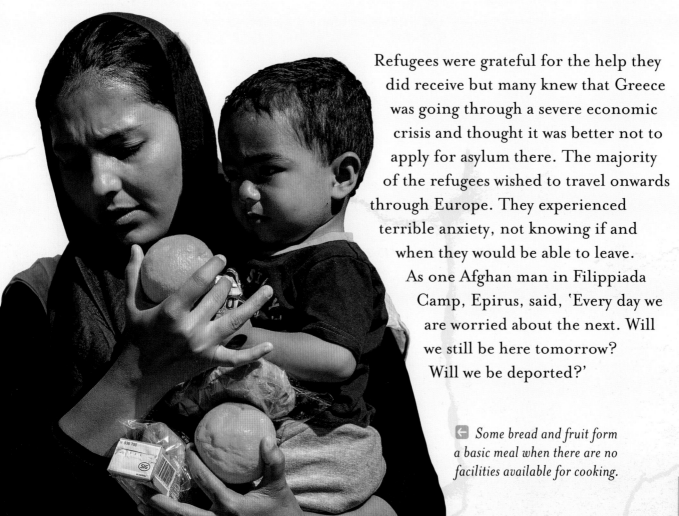

Refugees were grateful for the help they did receive but many knew that Greece was going through a severe economic crisis and thought it was better not to apply for asylum there. The majority of the refugees wished to travel onwards through Europe. They experienced terrible anxiety, not knowing if and when they would be able to leave.

As one Afghan man in Filippiada Camp, Epirus, said, 'Every day we are worried about the next. Will we still be here tomorrow? Will we be deported?'

Some bread and fruit form a basic meal when there are no facilities available for cooking.

31

↑ *After Hungary closed its border with Serbia, Croatia closed its borders with Serbia to stop refugees coming in.*

STRANDED!

Most refugees want to head where they think they will be welcomed. Germany and Sweden remain the favourite destinations because they have taken the most refugees and their economies are strong. Alternatively, refugees may wish to join relatives in another European country.

Once in Europe, thousands of refugees travelling onwards towards their hoped-for destination have reached borders, weary and desperate, only to find they have recently been closed. Countries are constantly changing their rules — shutting borders or introducing restrictions — so refugees have to find a different route.

↓ *The fence erected by Hungary along the border with Serbia.*

⬆ *While on the move, refugees communicate via WhatsApp or Viber.*

SOCIAL NETWORKS

There is a lot of information about refugees but little for them. Governments provide few details about safe routes to refuge because of fears this will encourage more to make the journey. Refugees have to rely on social networks for guidance. These networks are extremely important because many refugees choose to go it alone without paying people smugglers. Young, educated male Syrians who have reached their destination lead the way in passing on tips about routes to use and how to cross borders, setting up Facebook pages with maps and advice. They post updates on which countries have closed their borders to refugees and recommend alternative routes – if there are any.

'STOPPING THE FLOOD'

Until 2015, it was possible to travel through the Balkans: from Greece to Macedonia, Serbia and then Hungary, and on to northern Europe (see p 26). But in September 2015, Hungary erected a fence along its border with Serbia. Government spokesman Zoltán Kovács claimed, 'We need to stop the flood …' – to prevent migrants from reaching the rest of the EU. The Serbian government started to bus refugees to Croatia. Young, mobile male refugees tried out the new route first before families and those who travelled more slowly. They let others know via social media that the Hungarian-Serbian border was closed and they should head for Croatia.

TRAPPED IN GREECE

In October, Hungary built a fence along its border with Croatia, and Croatia said it would send refugees to Slovenia. However, in March 2016, Macedonia, Croatia and Slovenia closed their borders, so refugees could no longer travel from Greece to northern Europe. More than 57,000 refugees were stranded in Greece.

CASE STUDY Losing hope in Thessaloniki, Greece

In July 2016, Ruby, a 19-year-old student from Cornwall, UK **27**, travelled with her friend Jaime to Softex camp in Thessaloniki, Greece **28**, to support refugees who had been trapped there since the closure of the border with Macedonia in March.

The conditions were dreadful. Summer temperatures reached 40°C. Refugee families, including newborn babies, elderly and disabled people, were crammed into tents filling every corner of the camp. Dirt and dust were everywhere. People coughed continually, chest infections were common, and many children had caught conjunctivitis (an eye disease). With little to do, people grew stressed and bored, often leading to fights breaking out between young men.

Some refugees had endured these conditions for five months, and Ruby found they were falling into despair. 'No one was telling them when they would be relocated. They wondered how long they would remain there. Some had decided to return to Syria, saying, "Here I'm dying slowly. If I go back to Syria, at least my death will be quick".' Even the parents of young children had lost all hope.

The two young women delivered non-food items, such as nappies, to the tents. They learnt

a few words of Arabic, most of the refugees spoke a little English, and with the help of smiles, gestures and translation software they somehow communicated. Ruby felt her most important role was to spend time with people, to allow them to feel human again. One family, with five boys aged 2 to 12, said they only ever smiled when Ruby and Jaime entered their tent. Ruby was amazed at how welcoming they were, despite having so little. Whenever she visited, she was invited for tea.

➡ *The tents in Softex camp, one of the largest refugee camps in Greece, house more than 3,000 residents. Ruby found 16 people living in just one tent.*

To make a lasting difference, Ruby and Jaime raised around £1,600 through crowdfunding to establish a women's base, using the donations to reinforce the walls of a broken-down hut and buying rugs to make it comfortable inside. Refugee women set up a sewing space and an area for discussions, workshops and movie nights. The activities provided an element of control over their shattered lives as they waited and waited to continue their journey.

⬆ *In the winter, temperatures in Softex dropped to well below freezing, pipes froze and there was no running water.*

↑ *Refugees or migrants in Calais, trying to break into a lorry bound for the UK.*

THE CALAIS JUNGLE

Another place where refugees became stuck was Calais, northern France 29. Some had made an epic journey from distant Afghanistan, Sudan or Syria across Europe and through France. They hoped to reach the UK; many spoke English and some also had relatives there.

To get to the UK, refugees attempted to smuggle themselves into the back of a lorry bound for England. Night after night they waited for an opportunity. People smugglers carried tools to break into the back of lorries and let the refugees in, locking them in with little air, and no food or water. French police officers constantly patrolled to prevent illegal access to vehicles, and it became harder and harder to reach the UK without being caught.

THE STRUGGLE FOR SURVIVAL

Until October 2016, there were 9,000 people struggling to survive in the Calais community — the so-called 'Jungle'. They slept in tents; there was no running water or electricity, and it was bitterly cold in winter.

Various local and international grassroots organisations offered solidarity and support to the refugees of the Jungle. Elaine Ortiz from Brighton, England, set up the Hummingbird Project in 2015. Her volunteers drove to Calais regularly with nurses, support workers and 'everyday folk who really care' to cook food, offer first aid and medical services, and bring donated essential goods. They set up an art-led project in a 'safe zone' for under 18s, run by art psychotherapists and other volunteers. The sessions offered traumatised young people the opportunity to express themselves through painting and drawing.

CLOSING THE CAMP

In October 2016, the French authorities closed the Jungle completely and cleared the camp. Migrants were transferred to reception centres (temporary accommodation hostels) around France, where they were to be offered the chance to claim asylum — or face deportation back to their home country. The UK government paid for the construction of a 1-km-long wall along the main road to the port to prevent would-be stowaways from attempting to climb into lorries bound for England. For most of the migrants and refugees in Calais, their dream of reaching the UK was over.

>

FADING HOPES

In the first months you can feel the hope and energy and they'll say things like "see you in the UK". It's after six months that hope starts to fade.
Elaine Ortiz, Hummingbird Project

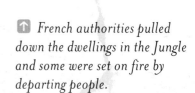

↑ *French authorities pulled down the dwellings in the Jungle and some were set on fire by departing people.*

← *Most people in the Jungle survived in tents or homemade shacks with very few possessions.*

➡️ *Conditions in the Jungle were harsh but at least volunteers could support the children, which became harder once they were sent away to different places.*

" POOR TREATMENT

They promised us they would take us to the UK but said we had to be patient. At this centre they treat us like donkeys. We are living in a factory and we are eating expired bread.

Teenager in a French refugee centre, 2017

THE DUBS AMENDMENT

In the UK, the Dubs Amendment to the 2016 Immigration Act allowed unaccompanied minors (child refugees) in Europe to be resettled in the UK. But only 350 children, later increased to 480, were to be accepted. Many children who applied were rejected.

UNACCOMPANIED CHILD REFUGEES

In 2015, 98,400 unaccompanied children lodged asylum claims (see page 41) around the world – the highest number ever. No one sends their child alone on a perilous journey unless it is the only option. Perhaps the families can only afford to give one member of the family the chance to escape the horrors of war. Other children are alone because their parents died on the way.

Most of the children who had reached the Jungle had experienced horrors in their home country and on the arduous trek to Calais. They shared the lack of food, money and shelter, as well as the trauma of the older refugees, but their age made them particularly vulnerable. When the Jungle was closed, the children were dispersed around France to refugee reception centres. They were promised they would still have a chance to come to the UK. But after it became clear that few children could come under the Dubs scheme (see panel), there was a surge of child refugees returning to Calais and Dunkirk, hoping to smuggle themselves to the UK. Without the child protection schemes that were available in the Calais Jungle, these children were targeted by people smugglers.

CASE STUDY **Abdul in the Jungle**

Fourteen-year-old Abdul was in the Jungle for a year, trying to sneak into lorries going to the UK. With no money to pay people smugglers, he put himself at even greater risk than most – he needed to avoid them as well as the police to enter a lorry. After one run-in with people smugglers, three of his refugee friends were hospitalised. Abdul was shaken up by the experience but remained determined to continue his attempts, saying he had absolutely nothing to lose. 'If I stay in the Jungle I might as well be dead,' he stated. Elaine Ortiz from the Hummingbird Project (see page 37) referred Abdul to be considered for resettlement in the UK under the Dubs Amendment, but he was rejected. As of late 2018, he remained in France.

⬆ *Most unaccompanied children in the Jungle were between 14 and 17 years old, but a very few were as young as eight.*

⬇ *At the Women's and Children's Centre, medical clinics, classes, social activities and women's clothes were available.*

REFUGEES WELCOME

↑ *German chancellor Angela Merkel was determined to make Germany a welcoming place for refugees.*

Canada and some European countries – notably Germany and Sweden – have been generous and welcomed many refugees.

ANXIETIES AND GUILT

Arriving after a horrendous journey, the experience for newcomers is bitter sweet. They are relieved to have finally reached a place of safety, but many have 'survivors' guilt' – they feel terrible about having survived when others perished on the journey. They are consumed with worry about their families back home and whether their relatives will be able to join them. They wonder how they will make a living. With all these anxieties, the reception they receive in their host country is hugely significant.

'WIR SCHAFFEN DAS'

In 2015, Germany took in 1 million refugees. Chancellor Angela Merkel announced to the world in August that *Wir schaffen das* – we can manage it. The following month, she allocated 6 billion euros (£5.2 billion) to support the new arrivals. Refugees are allowed to work, and as of August 2018, around 300,000 were in jobs.

More than 160,000 refugees sought asylum in Sweden in 2015, and all those who were granted a residence permit were offered a place to stay. Many NGOs and charities helped out, including Refugees Welcome, which connects refugees with landlords and flat shares. A group called 'Invitationsdepartementet' brings migrants and Swedes together over dinner so they can get to know each other.

ACROSS THE ATLANTIC

A few refugees have travelled even further from their homelands. As of February 2018, Canada had welcomed nearly 52,000 Syrian refugees. The government has assisted most of the Syrians to settle but nearly half are at least partly privately sponsored. Ordinary people have raised thousands of dollars to sponsor refugees. In more than 300 communities, Canadians have provided housing, English classes, dinner clubs and friendship to the newcomers. Between 2011 and 2018, about 21,000 Syrian refugees resettled in the USA.

APPLYING FOR ASYLUM

People who have made an independent journey to a safe country rather than a refugee camp in their home region need to make an asylum claim on arrival. In 2015, about 2.45 million applications were made, an increase of 48 per cent on 2014 and the highest number ever recorded. Syrians made the most applications.

CASE STUDY Zelga's story

Before the Syrian civil war broke out, Zelga Gabriel was a design student at Aleppo University. The conflict forced her to abandon her studies and return to her hometown. Zelga belongs to the Assyrian Christian minority. ISIS has targeted Assyrians for attacks, so her family made the heart-wrenching decision to leave. She says: 'If it was just up to me, I would never have left. Syria is my country; my roots are there. Some people say we weren't forced to flee Syria; that it was our choice to leave. But when you know that you might die at any time, then that *is* like you're being forced.'

⬇ *Zelga Gabriel in her adopted homeland, Sweden. She wants to study a subject such as psychology so that she can help other Assyrians in Sweden, or people back in Syria when she returns.*

➡ *The ancient Assyrian city of Nimrud, south of Mosul in Iraq, was destroyed by ISIS forces in 2015.*

Zelga had applied for a job in Sweden working with unaccompanied migrant children, so she had a far easier journey than most refugees. She travelled by bus and taxi to Lebanon and flew to Stockholm **30**. The journey took just a week. Arriving was a shock: 'When I first arrived and saw all the greenery, I was in tears. I felt like this place doesn't represent me and who I am, even if it's very beautiful.'

On arrival, Zelga applied for asylum. Most of her family members have settled with her in Södertälje **31**, where there is a large Assyrian community, and she spends most of her time with people from back home. She finds that Swedish people are different from Assyrians: 'There isn't as much connection between families. You don't meet your cousins that often, and you don't have time for yourself. You just work.' Although she is finding it hard to adjust, she wants to become part of Swedish society. She is making the effort to learn Swedish and adapt to the country that has offered her sanctuary.

ATTACKS ON CHRISTIANS

Before the civil war, Christians, including Assyrians, made up about 10 per cent of Syria's population. Iraq also had a sizeable Christian population. In areas of Syria and Iraq under ISIS control, ISIS leaders told Christians to convert to Islam or pay a special tax – otherwise they would face death. Hundreds of thousands of Christians have fled both countries as refugees.

↑ *Police patrol the Hungarian border fence to ensure refugees do not try to sneak in.*

↓ *Volunteers organised the distribution of pairs of donated shoes, offered to refugee children in the Hungarian capital, Budapest.*

WELCOMED BY THE PEOPLE

In some countries, including Hungary and the UK, government policy is not welcoming towards refugees, yet many ordinary people have stepped forward to assist them.

In Hungary, the government brought in harsh laws against refugees, making it illegal for Hungarians to aid them to travel to another European nation. Despite the law, thousands of Hungarians assisted them to travel across their country. Before the border was closed, volunteers collected crates of food and warm clothes for the newcomers. The Migrant Solidarity Group helped refugees to find a place to live and taught them Hungarian. However, in 2017, the government brought in a policy of detaining all asylum seekers and sending them back to neighbouring Serbia, so the group could no longer help refugees.

CASE STUDY Migrant English Project

As of March 2017, more than 6,000 Syrians had arrived in the UK through the Vulnerable Persons' Relocation Scheme, under which the UK committed to resettle 20,000 Syrians by 2020. Others have made their way through informal routes and applied for asylum. Whether or not they have achieved the legal right to be in the UK, refugees and migrants in Brighton and Hove are welcome to attend weekly English classes at the Migrant English Project.

It's Monday morning. At a small community centre, volunteers and students arrange tables and make coffee. The students arrive: long-settled migrants and refugees from South Asia and Ethiopia still studying to improve their English are joined by newer arrivals from Egypt and Syria, and a few eastern Europeans who are working in the city. People of all ages and from every continent are here. One couple, recently arrived from Syria, have come for the first time. They smile, but the pain and exhaustion are visible on their faces. No one needs to ask why they fled.

New students are matched up with teachers, and young children settle at the activity table. At lunchtime everyone eats a meal prepared by volunteers – sometimes students cook delicious dishes from their country. It's a chance to relax with a diverse bunch of people, a haven from the pressures of the outside world for students and volunteers alike.

➡ *An English class at the Migrant English Project, taught by volunteer teachers.*

World-famous scientist Albert Einstein left Germany when the Nazis came to power in 1933 and became a refugee in the USA. He made an enormous contribution to his adopted country.

REFUGEES: A BENEFIT TO SOCIETY

Many people believe that welcoming refugees is not only the right thing to do, but also that the newcomers bring lifeblood to the host country, contributing to the economy, society and culture.

Sweden and Germany both have a low birth rate. Their populations are declining and the proportion of elderly people growing; Sweden needs 64,000 working-age migrants a year to make up for its low birth rate. The German economy also depends on immigration — a 2017 report showed that the large numbers of migrants had allowed the economy to grow and led to high increases in employment for locals and refugees. There is evidence that refugees easily repay in taxes the costs of resettling them once they are working: they will repay EU spending on resettlement almost twice over in five years.

Syrian doctors who have fled their homeland are now treating patients in their country of refuge.

Syrian refugees are frequently highly educated and skilled professionals — doctors, dentists, teachers and engineers — who can fill skill shortages once they have mastered the language. Others set up their own businesses. They all spend money on goods and services, boosting the local economy.

CASE STUDY 'Germany's most popular refugee'

Refugees also bring their unique arts, music and culture. Aeham Ahmad is a musician from Yarmouk, a district of Damascus. In 2013, he placed his piano on a bombed street and, with a group of singers, began to play for his neighbours. His modest aim was to help keep them sane as they endured the fierce battles between government and rebel forces. Videos of Ahmad's appearances were posted online, giving a contrasting view of the war to the images of destruction, and he gained an international audience. But musicians in Ahmad's band were kidnapped, and his life was also in danger. Eventually, Ahmad escaped and fled to Wiesbaden, Germany **32**. There, he became known as the 'Piano Man of Yarmouk' and received invitations to play. Now he performs in a different city every night. He is grateful for his warm reception in Germany, but his heart remains heavy; he can't help thinking about friends and family he has left behind in Syria.

WHEN REFUGEES ARE NOT WELCOME

Not everyone is happy to welcome refugees into their country. Some fear that the newcomers will take their jobs and homes. They believe the cost of supporting refugees is too great a burden on the economy – the migrants will occupy precious school places and hospital beds. Surely it is more important to look after their own people? These issues are more serious in countries such as Lebanon, where refugees form a large part of the population.

Women who adopt the niqab, the face veil, may suffer from Islamophobic remarks or even be attacked.

Munich **33** reported customers cancelling sought-after places in beer tents because they were scared to mingle in large crowds in case of attack. In the USA, such incidents have affected government policy: following the discovery that two of the operatives involved in the terrorist attacks in Paris of November 2015 had posed as refugees, more than half of US states refused to take in people fleeing Syria.

DANGER FROM STRANGERS?

People who oppose accepting refugees sometimes say they are frightened of strangers — outsiders who do not speak the local language and follow a different religion — 'swamping' their culture. They feel their homeland will lose its traditions. Islamophobia — fear and dislike of Muslims — is particularly strong. Terrorist attacks in Europe, linked to the conflict in the Middle East and occasionally involving refugees, have fuelled these fears. Some feel that if Europe accepts refugees, it opens the gates to terrorists, intent on wreaking havoc. After a spate of incidents in Germany in 2016, the organisers of the traditional Oktoberfest beer festival in

Hate graffiti on the outside of a refugee centre in Lyon, France calling for 'migrants out!'

DONALD TRUMP AND REFUGEES

In March 2017, US President Donald Trump imposed a four-month ban on the resettlement of refugees. He feared that there was a risk of allowing terrorists into the USA and wanted to give his government time to check the vetting (checking) system for refugees. The courts overturned the ban, and around 50,000 refugees were allowed to come to the USA that year. Trump reduced the maximum to 45,000 for 2018 and planned to lower it to 30,000 in 2019. These figures were far lower than at any time since 1980. Many people felt it was unfair for the richest country in the world to accept so few refugees when poor countries were hosting millions.

49

OPPOSING VIEWS

A Pew Research Center survey in September 2018 showed the wide differences in views about refugees in ten European countries. In Germany and Sweden, four-fifths said that they would support taking more refugees. But in Poland, only half supported accepting refugees, while in Hungary, the figure was about a third.

EUROPE DIVIDED

As of September 2018, according to UNHCR, only 31 per cent of international funding required to help Syrian refugees and IDPs had been received. Greece, Germany, Italy and Hungary have high numbers of refugees and complain that other nations are not taking their fair share. Why should they shoulder the entire burden of the refugee crisis? Large numbers of people in European countries strongly disapproved of the way that the EU handled the 2015 refugee crisis.

⬇ *Emergency border controls introduced by Germany to control refugees entering from Austria, September 2015.*

SHUTTING THE GATES

In November 2015, Sweden ended its open-door policy because it was overwhelmed by 10,000 asylum seekers arriving every day. From 2016, refugees would receive only temporary residence permits and the number of family members who could join them was reduced. In 2017, the number of refugees arriving in Sweden dropped to around 25,600, the lowest figure in eight years. In Germany, emergency controls on the Austrian border were introduced in September 2015, because 63,000 refugees had arrived in a few weeks. Since then, thousands have been turned back at the Austrian border.

As the policies have changed in Sweden and Germany, the divide has grown between people who welcome refugees and others who campaign against them. In Sweden, far-right parties that campaign against all immigration – including refugees – are becoming more popular. In 2018, the anti-immigrant Sweden Democrats came third in the general election with 18 per cent of the vote. They want to stop Sweden receiving asylum seekers.

↑ *The far-right Nordic Resistance Movement protests against the 'invasion of strangers'.*

CHANGING CULTURES?

In Germany, welcoming attitudes towards refugees have also declined somewhat between 2015 and 2017. A survey showed that rising numbers believed that Germany had reached the limit in accepting refugees. The far-right gained ground here too: the Alternative for Germany entered Parliament for the first time in 2017. Yet the shift in opinions should not be exaggerated. On the whole, Germans remained positive towards refugees and a diverse culture, as did Swedes.

⬆ *A makeshift refugee camp in Greece on the border with Macedonia.*

KEPT OUT AND SENT BACK

Hungary has taken a tougher line. In March 2016 it closed the border to refugees coming from Serbia, declaring that Serbia was a safe country so there was no need for people to continue into Hungary. Of the 177,135 refugees already in Hungary in 2015 who claimed asylum, only 145 were granted permission to remain. After the border closure, those entering Hungary were sent straight to detention centres – places like prisons for detaining people who have entered the country illegally. In August 2016, Prime Minister Viktor Orban announced he was planning to build an even bigger fence than the first one to keep out refugees.

The European countries clubbed together to stem the flow of refugees. The border closures in Macedonia, Croatia and Slovenia of March 2016 closed off the Balkan route to northern Europe. In the same month, the EU made a deal with Turkey to stop the people

Refugees being returned from Greece to Turkey, August 2016. In February 2017, Turkish sources reported that 3,000 refugees had been returned from Greece to Turkey.

smugglers and to accept the return of refugees newly arrived in Greece from Turkey. One year later, the deal had failed, and most of the refugees — 62,000 of them — remained stuck in camps in Greece.

RISKY SEA ROUTES

Meanwhile, Middle Eastern and African refugees continued to escape to Greece, Italy and Spain. At reception centres in Spain, there was great sympathy for their plight. José Villahoz, president of an NGO that helps refugees, says they are used to migrants arriving and there's no need for alarm. Yet the situation is different in Italy, where the government is blocking aid to the refugees. In June 2018, it turned away a rescue ship, the *Aquarius*, with more than 600 migrants aboard.

More than 100,000 refugees and migrants arrived in Mediterranean Europe in 2018. Putting up fences, turning back boats or detaining refugees could not stop them. Such measures do not address the reasons why refugees flee in the first place.

DETENTION TO DETER

The Australian government deters refugees. It sends those who arrive without the correct documents to detention centres on Nauru and Manus Island in Papua New Guinea. Amnesty International documented that the conditions were horrific and that refugees were deliberately abused to try to deter others. Those granted refugee status may stay in Nauru or resettle in Cambodia, but the doors to Australia remain firmly closed.

Demonstrators protest in favour of allowing refugees to come to Australia, 2016.

CASE STUDY Shah's story

Shah came alone to the UK from Afghanistan when he was 18. When he arrived in the UK in a lorry, he didn't even know which country he was in. He just started to walk along the street, and a police officer asked if he had any identity papers – he didn't. The policeman was kind and took Shah to the police station, where an officer contacted the Home Office (the department in charge of migration). An interpreter helped Shah with the interview because he knew little English. He and his two fellow travellers stayed overnight in a cell.

The following day, Shah had an interview with a Home Office official, and was sent to Glasgow **34** to wait for his asylum interview. The asylum process was frightening and extremely stressful. Shah's asylum claim was refused, and he was terrified of being sent back to Afghanistan. His solicitor helped him to appeal. The young man had nightmares in which he received a letter saying his appeal had been turned down. One day, a large letter came through the door. Shah's heart was beating frantically. He read through the whole document and at the end it stated that he was

➡ *The aftermath of a Taliban suicide attack in Kabul, Afghanistan. In recent times, Afghanistan has suffered a devastating civil war. Its security forces continue to struggle to prevent the Taliban from launching attacks on innocent civilians as well as military targets.*

WHY SHAH FLED

'It's too young to be coming to a new country, but if you have a problem and you can't stay alive at home, that's the way it must be. [...] I had a big family, but unfortunately I lost most of them. Our problem was related to land, and there was violence – afterwards just me, my brother and my sister were alive. That's why I came here.'

allowed to stay: 'I feel like somebody saved my life. I called all my friends and told them. That was a good day. A very, very good day.' Shah was grateful to the Scottish Refugee Council and the other services that had helped him. Indeed, Scotland has done more than the rest of the UK to welcome refugees. Nine months after he arrived, he found a place at college to improve his English, and hopes to attend university. But his thoughts are always with his brother and sister in Afghanistan and he wonders how he could help them.

⬆ *Scottish people show their support for Syrian refugees. By December 2017, 2,000 refugees had arrived in Scotland.*

CONCLUSION: SAFE, LEGAL SOLUTIONS?

Charities including Oxfam and Save the Children have called for safe, legal routes to allow refugees to reach Europe.

⬇ *Refugees in Idomeni, Greece, in May 2016, wait to be taken to another place in Greece.*

AN OFFICIAL ROUTE

Patrick Kingsley argues in his book *The New Odyssey* that European governments should accept that it is impossible to completely seal Europe's borders. Desperate refugees will try to come whatever the rules so it would be best to create an official way. It would allow Europe to manage the flow, divide refugees fairly between countries and prepare facilities. With a population of more than 740 million in Europe, it should be possible to absorb the refugees. Non-European countries could also help. If some of the millions of refugees in the Middle East could go to Europe or other host countries, it would be easier for countries in the region to support the refugees who are left. Those refugees might stay in their host countries until they could be relocated, making the migration process simpler to organise.

⬆ *Arresting people smugglers will not stop refugees from attempting to flee from danger.*

BETTER ORGANISATION

A Syrian refugee commented, 'Why make us do all this trip? Just organise it: give people visas so they come on the plane.'

Such a policy fits with what refugees want. When Oxfam spoke to refugees in Greece in May 2016, they said that in the short term they wanted decent reception centres with adequate food and water, information about their rights and options, and education for their children. After that, they wanted to be allowed to move to a country with a stronger economy where they could find work or reunite with family members elsewhere in Europe.

↑ *2016: Iraqi soldiers retake the city of Fallujah from ISIS. Some refugees have returned to Iraq although the country is still in chaos.*

WISE WORDS

One Afghan refugee in Filippiada Camp, Epirus, Greece had a piece of advice: 'Divide us up among all of the countries so one country doesn't feel all the pressure. We don't mind. We just want to be able to go somewhere and live safely, in peace, so our children can have a proper education.'

A NEW LIFE

Some refugees are prepared to settle in another land. As of 2018, 35 states took part in UNHCR's resettlement programme. It transfers refugees from an asylum country to another where they can live permanently. Families are often selected because they have pressing medical needs that cannot be met in a refugee camp. In 2017, around 75,000 refugees departed for resettlement. It is not only those with medical problems that wish to move on. In Lebanon, many Syrians see little prospect that peace will return to their country in the near future and are considering relocating to Europe, Canada or Brazil.

NO EASY PATH

Resettlement is no simple option. Refugees often experience post-traumatic stress disorder. They may have other mental health issues or injuries to cope with, but need interpreters to help them to access health services. It is important to learn the local language, but even if refugees attend classes, this takes time, especially for adults. Children tend to pick up the language and make friends more easily at school, but adults may find it harder to make social connections and get to know local people, which can leave them feeling isolated.

GOING HOME

The vast majority of refugees want to go home eventually. Some go voluntarily although conflict still rages in their country. In 2017, 667,400 refugees went back, mostly to the Central African Republic, Syria and Afghanistan. Some Syrian refugees return from Jordan and Lebanon. One man took his family back from Za'atari, but regretted it once they had arrived because it was so chaotic and dangerous.

Prolonged conflicts make it extremely hard for refugees to return. When a long, complex war ends, a period of instability and uncertainty usually follows. No one should be forced to go back until there is genuine peace, which may take several years. The world has coped with huge refugee crises before, such as after the Second World War, and could do so again. No one chooses to be a refugee. Yet those of us who are not refugees do have the choice to offer sanctuary.

↑ *Refugees in Belgium, 1940. As of 2018, 65.5 million people worldwide had been displaced — more than in the Second World War.*

➡ *Most refugees prefer to return to their own countries to raise their children if they can.*

TIMELINE

2011
Civil war breaks out in Syria.

2013–14
The so-called Islamic State of Iraq and Syria (ISIS) seizes parts of Syria and Iraq.

APRIL 2015
More than 600 people drown when a boat capsizes crossing the Mediterranean from Libya.

AUGUST 2015
Germany opens its doors to Syrian refugees even if they have already set foot in another European country.

SEPTEMBER 2015
The image of three-year-old Syrian boy Aylan Kurdi, whose body is washed up on a Turkish beach, moves many Europeans to act to help refugees.

SEPTEMBER 2015
Hungary erects a fence and closes its border with Serbia.

SEPTEMBER 2015
Germany introduces border controls on the border with Austria to limit the number of refugees entering the country.

SEPTEMBER 2015
First Russian air strikes in Syria.

OCTOBER 2015
Hungary erects a fence along its border with Croatia.

NOVEMBER 2015
The European Union begins a scheme to relocate 160,000 refugees from Greece to other European states.

NOVEMBER 2015
Terrorist attacks in Paris, France by operatives linked to so-called ISIS kill 130 people.

NOVEMBER 2015
Sweden ends its open-door policy towards refugees.

GLOSSARY

AID
Money, food and other basic items sent to help countries in difficult situations.

ASYLUM
Protection given to people who have left their country because they were in danger.

ASYLUM SEEKER
A refugee who claims the right to live in safety in another country because of persecution in his or her own country.

BALKANS
The countries including Croatia, Bosnia and Herzegovina, Slovenia, Serbia, Montenegro, Kosovo, Macedonia, Romania, Bulgaria, Albania, Greece and part of Turkey.

BARREL BOMB
An oil drum or gas cylinder filled with explosives and dropped from an aircraft.

BIRTH RATE
The number of births every year for every 1,000 people in the population of a place.

BLACK MARKET
Illegal trade in goods, not controlled by government.

CASUAL JOB
Temporary work, such as harvesting fruit.

CITIZEN
A person with the legal right to belong to a country.

CIVIL WAR
A war between groups of people within the same country.

DETENTION CENTRE
A secure place, like a prison, used by some countries for detaining migrants who have entered the country illegally.

DISPLACED
Forced to leave home and move to another part of the country.

ETHNIC GROUP
A group of people who share a culture, tradition, way of life and sometimes language.

EUROPEAN UNION
An international organisation of 28 countries (27 when Britain leaves the EU) with joint economic, social and security policies.

FAR-RIGHT PARTY
A party that among other things believes only people whose families originally come from a country should live there, and that migrants should return to the country they came from.

HOMELAND
The country where a person was born.

HOMOPHOBIA
An irrational fear or dislike of LGBTI people.

INTEGRATE
Help to bring a group of people, such as refugees, into society.

INTERNALLY DISPLACED PERSON (IDP)
A person who has been forced to leave his or her home and move to a different part of the country.

ISLAMIST
To do with a religious and political movement that aims to run the political system and every aspect of life based on a literal understanding of the Qur'an. It is different from the religion of Islam.

ISLAMOPHOBIA
Fear and hatred of Muslims because of their religion.

KURDISH
Person from Kurdistan, a region stretching mostly across Iran, Iraq and Turkey. Iran and Iraq accept regions known as Kurdistan within their countries.

LGBTI
Lesbian, Gay, Bisexual, Transgender and Intersex. Intersex people have bodies that are not clearly male or female.

MIDDLE EAST
The name for the area of land

DECEMBER 2015
1 million refugees reach Europe in 2015.

JANUARY 2016
Turkey allows Syrian refugees to apply for work permits.

MARCH 2016
Macedonia, Croatia and Slovenia close their borders so refugees can no longer travel from Greece to northern Europe.

MARCH 2016
Turkey agrees to start taking back Syrian refugees from Greece.

APRIL 2016
Migrant arrivals in Greece drop by 90 per cent.

MAY 2016
In the UK, the Dubs Amendment to the Immigration Act is passed, allowing unaccompanied child refugees in Europe to be resettled in the UK.

AUGUST 2016
Prime Minister Viktor Orban of Hungary announces he is planning to build a bigger fence than the first one to keep out refugees.

AUGUST 2016
A refugee team competes in the Olympic Games in Rio de Janeiro, Brazil.

OCTOBER 2016
The French government closes the 'Jungle' refugee camp in Calais.

2017
More than 3,100 refugees and migrants die crossing the Mediterranean Sea.

APRIL 2017
Apparent Syrian government chemical attack against rebel forces in Idlib Province.

NOVEMBER 2018
The Syrian government has regained control of most of the country.

that stretches from the Mediterranean Sea to Pakistan, including Syria, Jordan, Israel, Lebanon, Saudi Arabia, Iran and Iraq, and sometimes Egypt.

MIGRANT
In this book, a person who moves across an international border to another country. It can also refer to a person who moves within their own country, such as a migrant from a rural to an urban area.

MIGRATION
In this book, the movement of people to another country. It can also refer to movement within a country.

MINIMUM WAGE
A wage fixed by the law as the lowest that should be paid to an employed person.

NON-GOVERNMENTAL ORGANISATION (NGO)
An organisation that is not part of government that works to help people and does not make profits.

PEOPLE SMUGGLER
A person who arranges for people to travel illegally to another country.

PERSECUTION
Treating people badly because of their ethnic group, culture, religious or political beliefs.

PORTABLE HOME
A building designed to be moveable, which is suitable for refugee camps.

POST-TRAUMATIC STRESS DISORDER
A medical condition in which a person suffers from psychological and emotional problems because of a difficult experience in the past.

PSYCHOTHERAPIST
A person who treats mental illness by discussing the problems with the patient rather than giving drugs.

PUBLIC SERVICES
Services provided by a government, such as healthcare, schools and policing.

RECEPTION CENTRE
A temporary home for asylum seekers while they wait for their asylum claim to be processed.

REFUGEE
A person who escapes to another country to seek safety from war, natural disaster or bad treatment.

RESETTLEMENT
When a refugee is transferred from the country to which he or she fled to another one, to live permanently.

RESIDENCE PERMIT
A document that allows people who are not citizens to stay in a country.

SPONSOR
A person or organisation that provides funds for a project, activity or a person.

STATUS, REFUGEE
When a person's asylum claim is accepted in a country and he or she has permission to stay, the person has refugee status.

TAXES
Money that you have to pay to the government so that it can pay for services, such as health and education.

UNACCOMPANIED MINOR (CHILD REFUGEE)
A person under 18, or the country's legal age for an adult, who has been separated from his or her parents and is not being cared for by another adult.

UNITED NATIONS HIGH COMMISSIONER FOR REFUGEES (UNHCR)
An international agency that works to protect the rights of refugees around the world, helping them to settle in the countries where they have sought asylum, resettle in other countries or to return home if it is safe to do so.

VISA
A stamp in a passport from a foreign country that gives you permission to enter, pass through or leave that country.

FURTHER INFORMATION

NON-FICTION BOOKS

Stormy Seas: Stories of Young Boat Refugees by Mary Beth Leatherdale and Eleanor Shakespeare (Annick Press, 2017)

Who are Refugees and Migrants? What Makes People Leave their Homes? And Other Big Questions by Michael Rosen and Annemarie Young (Wayland, 2016)

FICTION

After Tomorrow by Gillian Cross (Oxford University Press, 2013)

The Bone Sparrow: A Refugee Novel by Zana Fraillon (book: Orion, 2016/ audiobook, Hachette Children's Group, 2016)

Welcome to Nowhere by Elizabeth Laird (Macmillan Children's Books, 2017)

WEBSITES

Europe: don't let us down: Voices of refugees and migrants in Greece
https://www.oxfam.org/sites/www.oxfam.org/files/file_attachments/voices_from_greece_web.pdf Stories of refugee and migrant men and women in Greece

Migrant crisis: Migration to Europe explained in seven charts
http://www.bbc.co.uk/news/world-europe-34131911 Maps and graphics to explain the crisis

MIGRATION WATCH

https://www.migrationwatchuk.org
A UK organisation that is concerned about immigration to the UK

REFUGEE STORIES

http://scottishbooktrust.com/blog/reading/2015/09/refugee-stories
Refugees' own stories about moving to Scotland

SYRIA: A CHILDREN'S CRISIS

http://www.oxfam.org.uk/education/resources/syria
Oxfam site about how the conflict in Syria affects children

SYRIAN REFUGEES

http://www.pbs.org/newshour/tag/syrian-refugees/
From the USA, Public Broadcasting Service news about Syrian refugees

UNHCR KID ZONE

www.unhcr-centraleurope.org/en/general/get-involved/spread-the-word/education-resources-for-teachers/kid-zone.html
Games for children to help them to understand refugee experiences

FOR TEACHERS

In Search of Safety: Children and the Refugee Crisis in Europe
https://www.unicef.org.uk/rights-respecting-schools/wp-content/uploads/sites/4/2016/04/in-search-of-safety-complete-teaching-pack.pdf
Teaching pack giving the context of the refugee crisis, with 20 classroom activities to help children to understand it.

NOTE TO PARENTS AND TEACHERS:

Every effort has been made by the Publishers to ensure that the websites in this book are suitable for children, that they are of the highest educational value, and that they contain no inappropriate or offensive material. However, because of the nature of the Internet, it is impossible to guarantee that the contents of these sites will not be altered. We strongly advise that Internet access is supervised by a responsible adult.

BIBLIOGRAPHY

These are the main sources used for researching this book.

BBC, *'Exodus: Our Journey to Europe'*, Part 1, 2016

Kingsley, Patrick, *The New Odyssey: The Story of Europe's Refugee Crisis*, Guardian Books, 2016

Merits Partnership and Oxfam, *'Self-protection and coping strategies of refugees from Syria and host communities in Lebanon,'* 2015, *https://www.oxfam.org/sites/www.oxfam.org/files/file_attachments/rr-lebanon-refugees-protection-300616-en.pdf* Accessed 14 December 2016

Oxfam, *'Europe: don't let us down: Voices of refugees and migrants in Greece'*, 2016, *https://www.oxfam.org/sites/www.oxfam.org/files/file_attachments/voices_from_greece_web.pdf* Accessed 14 December 2016

UNHCR, *'Global Trends Forced Displacement in 2015'*, 2016, *http://www.unhcr.org/uk/576408cd7.pdf* Accessed 14 December 2016

CASE STUDIES

pp. 4–5 UNHCR; pp. 10–11 Jacob Kushner, *'The Brutal Consequences of Uganda's Infamous Anti-Gay Law'*, 17 March 2016, Vice Media, *http://www.vice.com/read/on-the-run-kenya-lgbt-v23n1* Accessed 6 September 2016

pp. 14–15 Clare Applewhite, author interview, September 2016

pp. 18–19 Human Rights Watch, *'When I Picture My Future, I See Nothing'*, 2015

pp. 20–21 Rana Husseini, *'Za'atari camp magazine gives refugees a voice'*, The Jordan Times, 25 January 2016 *http://www.jordantimes.com/news/local/zaatari-camp-magazine-gives-refugees-voice* and *'Refugee camp — our desert home'* BBC 2, 21 July 2016

pp. 28–9 Heather Saul, *'Yusra Mardini: Olympic Syrian refugee who swam for three hours in sea to push sinking boat carrying 20 to safety'*, The Independent, 5 August 2016 *http://www.independent.co.uk/news/people/yusra-mardini-rio-2016-olympics-womens-swimming-the-syrian-refugee-competing-in-the-olympics-who-a7173546.html* and Heather Saul, *'Yusra Mardini: Olympic refugee who swam for three hours to save 20 lives 'overwhelmed' by support'*, *http://www.independent.co.uk/news/people/yusra-mardini-olympic-refugee-who-swam-for-three-hours-to-save-20-lives-overwhelmed-by-support-a7182156.html* Both accessed 14 December 2016

pp. 34–5 Ruby Brookman Prins, author interview, September 2016

pp. 38–9 Elaine Ortiz, Hummingbird Project, author interview, September 2016

pp. 42–3 Nathalie Rothschild, *'Zelga Gabriel, Refugee from Syria'*, 12 April 2016, *http://www.nathalierothschild.com/2016/04/12/zelga-gabriel-refugee-from-syria/* Accessed 14 December 2016

46–7 Anne Barnard, *'From Syrian Rubble to German Concert Halls With a Piano, a Mission and Survivor's Guilt'*, New York Times, 6 August 2016, *http://www.nytimes.com/2016/08/07/world/europe/refugee-song-syria-germany.html?_r=0* Accessed 14 December 2016

pp. 54–5 Scottish Refugee Council, *'Shah's story'*, 2016

http://www.scottishrefugeecouncil.org.uk/what_we_do/refugee_stories/900_shahs_story Accessed 14 December 2016

63

INDEX